MW01199157

THE THREE LESSONS OF MR. MARKEW

How to turn dull talks into sparkling sermons

Graham Fysh

LifeTime Creations
Federal Way, WA

THE THREE LESSONS OF MR. MARKEW

Printed in the United States of America. No part of this book may be used or reproduced in any way without written permission except in the case of brief quotations embodied in critical articles or reviews. For information, write LifeTime Creations, 33602 27th Pl. S.W., Federal Way, WA 98023

Cover design by Fysh Quality Productions

Library of Congress Catalog Card Number 91-90056

ISBN 0-9628987-0-8

Published by LifeTime Creations, 33602 27th Pl. S.W., Federal Way, WA 98023-7711

CONTENTS

A Visitor

It was an essential Sunday morning routine, but shaking hands with more than a hundred people and mouthing the same platitudes always seemed an arduous duty to the Rev. Maurice Toblatt. Yet it had to be done.

This Sunday was as arduous as usual - until a short, balding, graying man he had never seen before came seemingly from nowhere, stepped in front of him, grasped his hand, shook it firmly twice, and asked: "I'm sorry to be so blunt, pastor, but how many people do you think will remember that sermon?"

Toblatt could not reply at first. Who could have?

As the man waited for a reply, Toblatt volunteered: "Quite a few."

The man took four or five sheets of paper from his inside jacket pocket.

"I've just polled them. I've been standing outside the main door over there and I asked each person I could catch what the main theme of your sermon was."

He looked down at his notes. "I must confess I'm not quite sure I know myself what the main point was, but I listened to your sermon quite carefully and I found only 5 percent even had the vaguest idea what it was about."

Toblatt was taken aback at the man's blunt approach.

"Well, Mr. ... "

"John L. Markew."

"Mr. Markew, you're probably right. But, you see, the purpose of a sermon is to leave an inspiring message. It's not a lecture. If I helped one person today to understand God - and themselves - a little better, I will have done my duty."

"I'm sure you're right, pastor. But I asked them, too, what they had learned from the sermon."

"Yes?"

"No one was so impolite as to say nothing, but a mere 8 percent replied in terms that fitted your sermon content. The rest replied with lessons that you had not even mentioned today - like ... " Markew consulted his notes. "Like, I should pray every day or I should love God, or I should love my neighbor."

"Mr. Markew, I don't know who you are, but I really don't know why you are telling me this."

Markew put away his notes.

"I'm here to challenge you, Mr. Toblatt. I want to suggest - quite humbly - that I can teach you in a week how to preach a sermon that will reverse these figures. Over many years of preaching and speaking in public I have developed techniques that can be used to turn dull sermons into absorbing dramas. After adopting the techniques I will demonstrate, I am prepared to predict that most of your congregation will go down those stone steps next week knowing what the main lesson of the sermon was.

"They will go home having learned something.

"The experience will have changed their lives.

"And they will have benefited so much they will tell their friends."

Markew was warming up to his theme.

"I am prepared to make this deal with you. You take my lessons this week and next week I'll take another poll and we'll compare the results."

Toblatt stepped back, tempted, but suspicious.

"Okay, Mr. Markew. What are you selling? What company do you represent? And how much does it cost?"

"I come only in love. And, if I may be so modest, I try to represent the Lord. My services are free."

It was not going to be as easy to get away as he had thought, reasoned Toblatt.

"Oh. Well, I'll think about it."

"My offer is for this week only. I have other churches to visit. How about every morning, Monday through Friday, for an hour each morning. Say, 9 to 10. In your church office."

The man's persistence was startling.

"Well, Monday's my day off and I promised to take my wife shopping tomorrow."

"Okay, just a greater challenge. How about Tuesday through Friday?"

"Well, I prepare my sermon on Fridays."

"And a mighty good one it's going to be this coming Friday. All right, Mr. Toblatt, you drive a hard bargain. Tuesday through Thursday. Three lessons."

How could he refuse?

Markew said he would be there Tuesday morning at 9.

Toblatt did not notice in which direction Markew had gone. And he realized only afterward that he had not obtained the man's address or telephone number, so he could not call to cancel.

First Lesson

Markew was in Toblatt's study at 8:58 a.m. on Tuesday. He was sitting in an easy chair. Toblatt assumed his wife had let Markew into the house.

"We're going to start with the opening of your sermon," Markew said, removing a rather worn notebook from his pocket. "Can you remember what you said at the outset of your sermon on Sunday?"

"Er ... I think I began by explaining that it was Palm Sunday - "

"With all respect, Mr. Toblatt, if you can't remember how you began, can you expect members of the congregation to do so?"

Toblatt had not expected to be cross-examined and did not know whether he liked it. But he listened on, thinking that perhaps he could learn something. After all, at the very worst he would waste three or four hours of his week.

"You see, pastor, the most important part of any sermon is the opening minute. You have 30 seconds to capture the attention of your hearers. If you fail to do so within that time, you will have to double your efforts in the next minute.

"If you fail again, the chances are you have lost them for the next 30 minutes.

"Therefore those first 30 seconds deserve intense examination. You need to practice precisely what you are going to say."

Toblatt leaned back in his chair. An interesting thought. But was it that vital? Sermons needed to be introduced. You needed to start off slowly.

"How can you be so sure of that?" he asked.

Markew felt a little explanation was in order at this stage.

"Let me explain myself. For 25 years I have wrestled with words to try to make them work effectively for me. Over that time, I have developed ways of speaking that I believe capture readers' attention.

"I based them on the techniques I saw used in television shows and in print. I found the same techniques being used over and over again. These could be translated into a number of key principles."

Markew picked up a copy of the newspaper.

"Writers have developed certain techniques because it is easy for readers to turn them off. They can throw down the newspaper or the magazine and that's that. They might even vow never to buy it again because it's so boring."

He pointed to a television set in the corner.

"Viewers can switch to another channel or hit the off switch.

"Your listeners do not do that. At least not immediately. They pretend to pay close attention. Some might even tell you later that your sermons are wonderful because they feel that is the right thing to say.

"But the effect is the same as bored newspaper readers and television viewers who tune out. The only difference is that it is more gradual. Your listeners do not get up and walk out. Some simply stay away after time. Others continue to come because they believe that going to church is part of their duty. But they are reluctant to invite others.

"The result is that your church will not grow if your sermons are dull. That is your Nielsen rating. People turn you off by not coming."

Toblatt found himself becoming interested in what Markew was saying. It made sense. He nodded.

One of the key techniques that is common to newspapers, television, radio and good preachers is that they attract their audience at the outset, Markew explained.

Media experts call this the hook, he added.

"But you cannot know how to start your sermon until you know what its theme is going to be. So I'm going to talk today about the central theme of your sermon because the opening 60 seconds must be structured on that theme."

"And every sermon must have a central theme."

Toblatt nodded. That was pretty obvious.

Markew wrote THEME on his notebook and held it up.

"At some stage you are going to have to develop a paragraph that summarizes the whole emphasis of what you are trying to say.

"This is not the first paragraph. It's not that arresting opening I was discussing earlier. We'll get to that tomorrow.

"It's the central pivot around which your whole sermon rotates."

Markew waved his notebook at Toblatt. "May I suggest you take notes? It will help you to remember these points."

Toblatt pulled open a drawer and took out a pad and pencil.

"It might be an idea to have your congregation take notes, too. You can provide outlines like this one."

Markew handed Toblatt a copy of a "Sermon Notes" form.

"That will help them concentrate on what you are saying and will provide a useful reference to which they can refer.

He suggested, too, that Toblatt might like to have an outline of his main points projected on to a screen, much like the words of songs are projected on overhead projectors at many churches. The total outline could be covered over at the beginning and, as he reached each point, an assistant would remove the covering to reveal that point.

The congregation would tend to write down the outline on their note forms, much as students write down what lecturers write up on the chalkboard.

"To return to the theme," continued Markew. "It has to follow certain basic guidelines.

"The first is that it should contain a verb."

Toblatt wrote that down. What Markew said made sense and he was beginning to feel that maybe this exercise would be of help to him, after all.

"Why a verb?" he asked. "This is not a written article."

"Aha," replied Markew. "You're responding. That's good. And it's a good question, too.

"The reason for the verb has nothing really to do with grammar. Its purpose is that it forces you to make a statement.

"I must confess that I have spent many bored hours in pews listening to sermons that are ABOUT something. If the preacher really had to think about it, he would have to admit that his theme was about Christian love or about giving or about prayer ... or whatever.

"For example, you might say that your sermon on Sunday was ABOUT Palm Sunday. Quite frankly, that's all I could be sure it was about.

"But, you see, that statement does not contain a verb and therefore it tells me nothing. I'm not likely to go home and tell my wife: You should have come to church, dear. We heard a good sermon about Palm Sunday.

"She's likely to respond: But what about Palm Sunday?

"If you put a verb in it, your theme is going to start to live and breathe. If you tried to develop a theme around the Palm Sunday story and you made sure it had a verb in it you might come up with something like: This week, take your worship from the church into the world outside.

"That verb is already starting to work for us.

"By forcing ourselves to prepare a statement with a verb in it as a theme, we are forced to say something definitive."

Toblatt had to confess to himself that Markew's initial comment on his theme was indeed the one he had written down for the sermon. It was ABOUT Palm Sunday.

The next step, continued Markew, is to take that verb and make it stronger. Developing a strong verb will make the sermon's theme more vital and more meaningful. Instead of "take your worship," he suggested, you might say "carry your worship from the church into the world outside."

Or, "transfer your worship from the church into the world outside."

"As you work at it, you will find the verb really working for you," explained Markew. "And it will provide you with different nuances of meaning. Continue thinking of verbs - use a thesaurus if you like - to make sure you find exactly the right one to convey the meaning and the impact you want."

"Now you suggest a theme," continued Markew.

Toblatt thought for a while. He tried to recall some of the points that he had noted down for his sermon on Sunday.

"Well, Palm Sunday shows us that Jesus was not an earthly king. "

"That's still not quite right, I'm afraid."

"It has a verb," Toblatt replied.

"Yes, but it breaks the second rule to which I was coming. That is, the theme should never be negative.

"People get bored when you tell them what is not true or what did not happen. I could tell you about all the aircraft that did not crash yesterday and you'll probably be bored. But let me tell you about the one that did crash and your interest will be sparked.

"The point here is not that we should tell people about disasters, but that we should tell our listeners something out-of-the-ordinary, something new and unusual that we believe they need to know."

Toblatt begged to disagree.

"What if I want to tell my congregation that they should not gossip about their neighbors or that they should not cheat on their business dealings?"

"Tell them, by all means, but that should not be the theme of your sermon. The first could be structured around that great commandment: Love your neighbor. Pretty positive. By all means, mention the importance of not indulging in gossip as one of your points, but don't make it your theme paragraph.

"Your second example about not cheating could be built around the theme: Examine yourself to find out whether you are showing honesty in business dealings.

"It's a matter of words, but words are important. It's not always what you say as much as the way you say it, remember. Even if you are getting across a negative point - like the examples above - put it in positive language."

Toblatt took notes.

"Next point about that theme paragraph. In addition to containing a verb and being positive, it should be something that your readers - or listeners - are unlikely to think of for themselves.

"It should be fresh, new and challenging.

"I think you can assume that your congregation has heard of the commandment to love their neighbors. That's why I suggested the theme be structured around that commandment, not necessarily consist of it. But you need to come up with something new about it. That's where your expertise as a theologian comes in. You have the training to be able to do that. Use that training."

Shaking his notebook to indicate that Toblatt should take notes, Markew continued: "Now for the final point about the theme.

"It must be concise.

"This means, too, that it should not be too complex. Obviously, it's not much good coming up with a trite point that is nothing more than a cliche or a platitude. But don't turn it into a thesis. Make it meaningful and make it brief.

"Summarize and summarize until you are able to do that. Work at it. Your theme, or nut graph, is a vital element of your sermon. It's the heart of your sermon. Neglect it and your sermon will die of heart failure.

"Let's see your notes."

Toblatt held up his notebook.

The theme

Every sermon must have one.

It must:

1. Have a verb.
2. Be positive.
3. Say something fresh and new.
4. Be concise.

The heart of the sermon. Work at it.

Heart Beat

"You're learning well, Mr. Toblatt. Those notes are good. Keep them. Refer to them whenever you prepare a sermon until they are a part of you. Of course, this is only the start. That is only one element of your sermon. But it's one of the most important structural elements. It's the pivot on which the whole sermon rests. It cannot survive without it.

"For that reason, never be satisfied until the theme of your sermon - the nut graph - meets all those requirements that you have written down.

"Come back to the nut graph as you work through the sermon. New ideas, new thoughts, will strike you as you prepare the body of the sermon. When they do, look at that nut graph again and rework it. It must reflect the essence of what you want your congregation to take away with them, therefore your whole sermon should be structured around it.

"And remember that each sermon has ONLY ONE THEME. Be satisfied with getting one point across each Sunday. If your congregation remembers that, and they come to church once every Sunday, they will have 52 points worth thinking about each year. That's 104 nuggets of truth in two years.

"At present, they are probably remembering only 10 percent of that - 5.2 points a year - if that."

Toblatt leaned back in his chair and coughed. He was intrigued by what he had heard and he wanted to know more.

"Er ... " He coughed again. "How do you choose a subject, Mr. Markew?"

"Excellent question. How do you decide what that theme is going to be?

"Again, I'm going to lean on my study of the media to indicate where I got many of my ideas for sermon themes.

"A way the media get ideas for stories is from people who call in with suggestions. Someone will call in and say there have been a lot of fires in our area recently. An arsonist could be at work.

"Those tips for you come from your congregation. Has anyone in your church body been wrestling with a problem lately? Has anyone asked you a question? Perhaps someone has commented to you about a situation a friend is facing. All these are possible subject areas.

"When you prepare your sermon this Friday, write down some of the things people have told you that week. There might be material there. If you don't use it this week you might use it another week. Place the ideas in a special folder. Call it:

Sermon ideas.

"Another avenue for media stories are regular checks. Reporters call the police, the ambulance services, the hospitals and the courthouses to find out what they have been doing. Often what they are doing is news.

"Your version of those are the organizations within your church - the women's association, the youth league, the choir. Make it your business to find out what has been happening there. Not only is this a good practice for your general ministry, but good sermon topics could be lurking there.

"Perhaps Mrs. Jones in the choir has had to leave because she cannot attend practices on Thursday evenings. You learn she is working nights to earn more money. There might be a sermon in that. Without mentioning her name, or making even an indirect reference to her, you could choose as a sermon theme: Serving God is more important than making a lot of money. That's provocative and could be a challenge to many in your congregation. Of course, that does not mean you need to condemn Mrs. Jones. Her circumstances might be special and you, too, might advise her to take the second job. But the important thing is that it has given you a peg for a sermon theme.

"Another source of news is simply reading newspapers or watching television to find out whether there are news items that are worth following up. You should do that, too.

"Many in your congregation follow the daily news. They would like to hear your comments on

it. Talk about AIDS and the resulting impact on sexual mores and you will have the ear of everyone in your church. You can ignore the world outside in your sermons, but you do so at your peril. After all, your congregation lives with it every single day.

"Also, consider holidays as a source for themes. For example, the Sunday closest to Veterans' Day could yield a sermon that discusses if, when and how Christians should be involved in war.

"Notice that in all cases I'm suggesting you choose sermon themes from matters that concern your congregation - questions they are asking, things happening to them and their friends, events taking place around them.

"Start with the people themselves. Don't start with yourself.

"Ask: What interests them? Not: What interests me?"

Toblatt nodded. He picked up his pen again and made some notes.

Markew noticed.

"You're taking notes. That's great.

"Another major source of news is usually called the futures file. Whatever you call it, it consists of a file in which items worth covering are stored under the dates on which they are likely to occur.

"For example, a politician says in November that he will announce whether he is going to run for mayor on February 15. A bright city editor drops a note in his futures folder under February 14: Check tomorrow to see whether Jones will run for mayor.

"Your equivalent?"

"Well," said Toblatt, warming up to the idea, "I suppose that would be events occurring in the church calendar."

"That's a good idea," replied Markew. "In your local calendar, and possibly in the general church calendar. A world day of prayer for missionaries in which your church is participating, for example, could get special treatment from you in a sermon.

"One final source of news I will mention here is the files - clippings from old newspapers, items recorded years ago. For example, a glance at a newspaper a year old will show that a major earthquake occurred exactly 365 days ago next week. A reporter could prepare a story for use on the anniversary day on what the people in the city are doing now. What provision have they made should another earthquake occur? How are those who lost loved ones in the earthquake faring now?

"Similarly, an editor might just page through an old newspaper for ideas. Stories written then might spark ideas for stories that can be written now.

"Your equivalent of that is ... "

Toblatt suggested it is the Bible.

"Of course," said Markew. "I don't have to tell you this is your main reference book, your main source, and you need to refer to it continually in the preparation of your sermon. I assume you are using it now for sermon topics. Most pastors do.

"Opening the Bible to any passage could give you a sermon idea. Another effective way to use the Bible for sermon topics is to go through it systematically. Select a book, start at the beginning and each week select a group of verses for your text, and, of course, your theme. You could take a year to work through a whole book."

Markew waved his notebook at Toblatt. "Let's see your notes so far."

Sermon ideas:

1. Tips from congregation - questions asked. comments made.
2. Organizations within church - what are people in them doing?
3. Newspapers or television - what are people out there talking about?

Ask: What interests them? Not: What interests me?

4. Holidays or special church days.
5. Future events on church calendar - keep a file.
6. The Bible - select a verse at random. or work through a book.

R&D

Markew smiled.

"Excellent," he commented. "What more can I say?"

"Before I leave today, I want to talk about another essential element of your sermons - research.

"This goes hand-in-hand with the central theme, but is a distinctly different aspect of it."

Toblatt waved his hand around his study. On one wall, bookshelves, filled with theological works, stretched from the floor to the ceiling. Against another, a freestanding bookshelf held a series of biblical encyclopedias.

"That's no problem," he said. "I've got all the facilities I need for research right here."

"That's good," Markew replied. "But does your congregation know or care?"

"What do you mean?"

"Well, I became a family joke many years ago after I bought the Encyclopedia Brittanica. I proudly displayed the books in my living room and showed them to everyone who was interested - and everyone who was not interested, too.

"One day an uncle of mine, after examining the books and hearing my enthusiastic recital of what they contained, asked how many of the books I had read.

"I told him I had read none. After all, one does not really read encyclopedias, does one? They are there for reference.

"My uncle smiled. So you think that by simply having them on display you have become a much wiser person, he said. But all that knowledge in all those books is going to be of little use to you unless you absorb it and put it into your head.

"He was right, of course.

"And this is, as you know, particularly true of the Bible. Many people walk around with Bibles under their arms, but how often do they read them?"

Toblatt removed one of the books from a shelf. It was worn and clearly well used.

"Again, no problem with that, here," he said. "I refer to these books constantly. Some, of course, I use more often than others. Like this one. It's a Bible commentary that has stood me in good stead for many years."

"Wonderful. But are you really finding out things that your congregation wants to know about?"

"Certainly. Understanding the text helps me understand the meaning of the passage and I can pass that meaning on to my congregation."

"Well said. I will not quarrel with that. But the research of which I am talking concerns illuminating the nut graph. Once you have decided the theme of your sermon, you need to work toward expanding on it.

"And that does not mean illuminating only the subject itself, remember. It does not mean looking up all the references you can find to Palm Sunday, because your theme is not Palm Sunday - it is something with a verb.

"Let us say you decide to take as your theme: We should carry our worship of the Lord from the church into the world outside, just as those people did on Palm Sunday.

"The purpose of your research will be to illuminate that subject - ways in which we can worship the Lord everywhere. You will want to know the different ways of worship. You'll want some details of each. You may not want to discuss the specific details of each in your sermon, but it will be good for you to know them so that you have a broad area on which you can draw.

"By the way, all that business about the best sermons being divided into three parts is absolutely true, at least as far as my studies have shown. Many authors on writing have noted that three is the best number - for dividing up a story, for points made within a sentence, and so on. Four is too many, two is too few. Try to keep to three major points whenever you can."

Toblatt put down the book.

"Well, at least something I was taught seems to be correct in your assessment," he commented.

"I'm sure, Mr. Toblatt, that it is all true to some extent. I'm not trying to encourage you to throw all your years of theological training out the window. I'm trying to help you to communicate more effectively. I'm trying to show you how to use that knowledge you have acquired to better purpose.

"You see, we might know all there is to know. But that does not mean we can pass it on. We've all encountered those professors who are brilliant in their field, but are quite useless when it comes to teaching others.

"Yet the ability to communicate often consists of knowing just a few secrets, such as those I'm trying to pass on to you. Apply those keys and the door of effective communication will open to you.

"By all means use that research ability you have been taught. But learn to communicate that knowledge you have acquired and will continue to acquire each week as you prepare your sermon."

Markew leaned forward.

"How do you research your sermon now?"

"I use Bible dictionaries, commentaries and many of these top scholarly works I have here." Toblatt again waved his hand around his study.

"Good. Use them. But - and this is important - make sure you are relating what you find out to ordinary people. We're simple folks out there, Mr. Toblatt. We don't come to church to learn about complex theological issues. It's your job to know all about those complex issues, but to translate them into things we can use in our everyday lives.

"Is that all the research you do?"

Toblatt frowned. Was there any other?

"Why, yes," he replied. "I spend quite a lot of time on it, too."

"Good. There is another form of research from which I think you could benefit.

"Research through interviews.

"Say a reporter wants to know the latest unemployment figures for a particular area and they are so new they have not been published in any reference books yet. He or she calls the Bureau of Labor Statistics and gets them."

Markew stood up, walked to the window and looked out.

"Out there, Mr. Toblatt are thousands of people who can help you with up-to-date information on a score of subjects that you can use as illustrations in your sermons. They are only a telephone call away.

"Want to know the inflation figure in order to illustrate a point in your sermon? Don't guess. Call up someone who knows.

"Want to know more about a subject you are discussing, but of which your knowledge is hazy? Call the people who know. Interview them. They will be only too pleased to tell you.

"You might have people in your church - elders, perhaps, or members - who can give you information about their daily work that relates to Christian principles. It could give you a whole new perspective."

Markew walked back to his chair. He spotted a newspaper lying on Toblatt's desk and picked it up.

"Your daily newspaper and news magazines are valuable sources of research for you. Keep files on subjects you know you will probably discuss - and place the clippings in them.

"Such a subject

might be crime. Whenever there is a story on the crime rate or a change in crime patterns, clip it out and throw it in your crime file. When you get to discuss crime in your sermon, you can talk authoritatively, from the recent clippings.

"I'm about to leave you," he said, standing once more, "but before I go I want to see the notes you have made on those last points."

Toblatt held up his pad. He was getting used to this now.

Research:

Illuminate your theme by using research

1. Research the theme - the nut graph - not the subject.
2. Three remains the best number of points for a sermon.
3. Use scholarly works, but relate findings to ordinary people.
4. Interview experts to get a new perspective.
5. Keep files of clippings to illustrate topics.

Crash Course

The sound of the crash made Toblatt jump. It had been preceded by a screech of brakes and must have come from the main road that ran past his church office. The traffic was fairly busy at 9 a.m. on a Wednesday.

He went to the open window and moved the drapes so he could see the road. But the traffic was moving smoothly and he could see no signs of a crash. That was strange. He was convinced the sound had come from this direction.

Toblatt opened the window and peered to the right and to the left, as far as he could see without going outside.

No signs of any pile-up.

As he turned to return to his desk he received an even greater fright than that given him by the sound of the crash.

Markew was sitting at his desk.

"Aha. Got your attention didn't it?"

"I don't understand. The sound of the crash ... "

Markew held up a tape recorder.

"It was on here. I put the machine outside the window."

Toblatt smiled. He had certainly believed it was the real thing.

Markew stood up and walked toward Toblatt.

"Last year, that was the last sound that 35 people in this community - in the area served by your church - heard in this life. People you could have reached. Perhaps you know of one or two. The rest were lost - gone from this earth - before you could speak to them. They might have needed to hear your message, but they did not.

"Isn't it time you did all you could to reach those who are still alive today, but might not be tomorrow?"

Markew had reached Toblatt and was looking him straight in the face.

Suddenly he stepped back and stretched out his hand, inviting Toblatt to sit down at the desk.

"That demonstration had two purposes, Mr. Toblatt.

"One, I was showing you the effectiveness of gaining a person's attention right at the outset. Because of that tape recording and your reaction, you were ready to hear what I had to say.

"I dare say you will remember that little sermonette because it followed a dramatic introduction. You might even tell your friends about it because it is unusual.

"And the whole thing took less than two minutes. My little sermon took less than a minute.

"But you'll probably remember that long after you've forgotten a hundred dull, boring 30-minute sermons with endless moralizing and no life to them."

Toblatt was not sure how to react. But he realized lesson number two had started. He glanced at his watch. It was 9:03 a.m.

Markew sat down in the visitor's chair and continued the lesson.

"Yesterday I emphasized the importance of gaining your listeners' attention right at the outset - in the first 30 seconds if possible. Then I went on to discuss the central theme and research.

"Today I want to return to the start of the sermon.

"The reason I have adopted this order is that this is the way you should prepare your sermon. Start by preparing the nut graph, or theme statement, continue into your research - and then decide how you are going to launch your sermon.

"You need to start with something arresting - something that will attract the attention of your listeners.

"When you started your sermon on Sunday by saying: Today is Palm Sunday and so I'm going to talk about the events of that day and ... you had already lost more than half your congregation. What's so interesting about that? And it's not even a proper theme.

"And my suggested topic: We should carry our worship of the Lord into the world outside is not, in itself, strong enough to start your sermon. It's a theme, but it does not belong in first place, It's the kernel, or nut, around which the whole sermon is built.

"Your sermon starter needs something better than that.

"You need to make your listeners sit up and take notice."

Markew referred to his clippings once more.

"My study of the media showed me that most successful newspaper stories or TV shows start with something with which you can identify. For example, a story about lower interest rates will start with a story of a couple who are struggling to meet their mortgage payments each month.

"I asked an editor of a financial magazine how he succeeds in making his articles relevant to the average reader - and to keep them returning month after month. He said the secret was to use examples from the community.

"You can do the same. You need to start with something to which people can relate - a story they will be interested in. Of course, it must relate to the overall theme of your sermon. Then, with the use of a transition, you glide into the main point - the nut graph, or the theme."

Markew explained that he had found that some newspaper and television stories started with an anecdote, or brief story, that gained the attention of readers or viewers. Others started with what he called a scene setter - placing the reader or viewer at the scene.

"Both serve the same purpose. They help get the reader into the story in an interesting way.

"You can do the same. Start with an anecdote or a scene setter that will seize the imagination of your listeners.

"And let me emphasize the importance of trying to find something to which your listeners can relate. Start from the known and move into the unknown. Don't tell a story about a situation that is totally foreign to your people. They must be able to visualize themselves in the situation.

"One of the most memorable sermons I have ever heard started with the minister suggesting we close our eyes and imagine we were on a beach. He told us of the sights we were seeing and the sounds we were hearing.

"The whole congregation was with him on a beach. He had their undivided attention."

Toblatt took up the notebook he had been using on the previous day and made some notes. Markew nodded appreciatively.

"Good sermons - like newspaper articles or television shows - can be started in a variety of ways, but they all boil down to one aim: To gain the listener's attention," Markew continued.

"Your listeners have a lot on their minds. They're thinking of bills that have to be paid, of what they face when they get to work the next day, of Aunt Nelly who is ill in the hospital, or of their son who told them in no uncertain terms why he was not going to go to church that morning.

"You cannot compete with that by saying: Today is Palm Sunday ... They might not deliberately turn you off, but those other thoughts will soon start to crowd you out. Their minds will wander off in search of greener pastures of thought.

"So you jump in first. You have some help. You have them looking at you. That's a start. You have silence. That helps. You have 10 seconds of grace in which you have their undivided attention. That's a bonus.

"Now seize the moment.

"Use those 10 seconds to win another 30 seconds for yourself. Then use those 30 seconds to secure another minute - and so on.

"Do not let it drag.

"A good editor on a newspaper is one who knows how to cut the fluff out of copy. A skilled editor can trim an overwritten 15-inch story into a 5-inch story and effectively lose nothing.

"Cut the fluff out of your sermon."

Markew reached on to Toblatt's desk and took the Bible off it.

"Let's see how the master preacher did it."

He turned to Mark chapter 12, verse 1: "He then began to speak to them in parables."

Markew looked up at Toblatt.

"I don't have to tell you how often Jesus used parables. Remember the stories of the sower of the seed, of the vineyard, of the prodigal son. Matthew 13:34 says: ... He did not say anything to them without using a parable.

"A parable is an anecdote. That is the way Jesus gained the attention of his hearers.

"It was highly effective then. It is highly effective now.

"Notice, too, the way in which Jesus captured the attention of his listeners when he did not use parables.

"Remember the woman caught in adultery and brought to him? John chapter 8 tells us that, after taking a few seconds to find out what the trouble was, he turned to the crowd and challenged them: If any one of you is without sin, let him be the first to throw a stone at her.

"He challenged his audience in an unusual yet highly effective way. He did not sit them all down and give them a long dull talk on the morality of stoning people. As a result, what he said has been quoted down the corridors of time.

"On another occasion, when asked whether it was right to pay taxes, Jesus asked his listeners to give him a coin. He asked them whose head they saw on it.

"You remember that story. Jesus related what he was saying to something the people knew. They all used coins every day of their lives. They all knew that Caesar's head was on the coins.

"Give to Caesar what is Caesar's, said Jesus, and to God what is God's. He got his point across highly effectively by reaching people at their level. So many of us, I'm afraid, would have answered that question - meant to trick him - with a long diatribe on the meaning of taxes, the state and the law. We would have lost our listeners within a few minutes.

"Jesus was so effective in his reply that these words, again, have been quoted down the centuries."

Toblatt nodded. It made sense. He took more notes.

"Jesus also used the anecdote of the Good Samaritan to illustrate his answer to another question.

"When the man wanted to know who his neighbor was, Jesus told him in the form of a story. I'm sure I don't have to repeat it.

"At the end, he asked: Which of these three do you think was a neighbor to the man who fell into the hands of the robbers?

"The man said the one who showed mercy.

"Jesus drives home the point of the story with one statement: Go, and do likewise.

"So many preachers seem to think that they have to say the same thing over and over again. They seem to believe that one needs 10 minutes to make one simple point. Jesus did it in 12 seconds. And the world is still talking about it.

"Notice, too, that the story, or anecdote, took a whole lot longer to tell than the message. The story takes six verses of the Bible and the message takes two.

"You can use stories like that in two main ways.

"The first we have already discussed. Use an anecdote - a brief story - to gain your listeners' attention. Don't waste a single word. Jump into it and stake a claim to their concentration with a powerful story told simply and quickly right at the outset.

"The second way is that, as you work your way through the main points of your sermon, you should illustrate what you have to say with anecdotes.

"Indeed, I would go so far as to say that every important point you make should be illustrated in at least one way.

"Illustrate, illustrate and illustrate.

"Your listeners will remember the illustration long after any moralizing from you. But the illustration will make them remember the point."

Markew stood up and walked to the window.

"You see, Mr. Toblatt, we pattern our lives largely after the experiences of others. If we admire a lawyer, we consider becoming lawyers ourselves. We do not usually consider becoming lawyers because someone wags his finger at us and tells us we have to do so.

"That's why television commercials so often include a person telling of their experiences in using a product. That's essentially a story of someone who has had good results from the product. The hope is you will be convinced to buy it because others have.

"We have a superb product. And the best way to prove the effectiveness of the product is is to illustrate what we say with examples."

Markew sat down again and leaned forward.

"I don't want to embarrass you, Mr. Toblatt, but about the only detail I really remember from your Sunday sermon was when you referred to an article in the Jerusalem Post. You held up the newspaper and told us that the story referred to Russian Jews returning to Israel. You related this to prophecy.

"I remember that because it was an example, an anecdote. And you held up a paper, which gained my attention. Unfortunately, however, that had nothing to do with the main theme of your sermon, which was something about Palm Sunday. And it came so late in the sermon you had already lost my attention for the earlier part.

"You see, the visual aid worked. But it did not work effectively for you, because it came so late and because you did not relate it to the theme of your sermon."

Toblatt nodded. He put down his notebook and looked up at Markew.

"Yes, I understand what you are saying. I just added it as a point of interest. It was not really related to my theme. But then I must confess my theme was vague. I did not really know what it was myself. You've already explained why that was wrong.

"But I'm only an ordinary person. I don't have a whole bunch of exciting stories ready to throw at people and keep them riveted to their pews.

"I've had a pretty straightforward life. About the most exciting thing that has happened to me was when I had a flat tire in the middle of a snowstorm."

Markew smiled.

"No problem. Most of us are like that, Mr. Toblatt. And if we have had one or two dramatic experiences, our listeners are soon going to become tired of hearing them recited over and over again.

"You don't have to experience the events yourself to tell about them. Jesus did not say how he got the story of the Good Samaritan, but he did not include himself in it. It was a story.

"Anecdotes - illustrations - are easy to find.

"May I suggest you get yourself folders, mark them with general subject headings, and file each anecdote.

"You'll find them in the newspaper every day - the odd story that catches your attention and that you realize can be adapted to make an important spiritual point.

"That's an excellent source. So are magazines - news magazines, general interest magazines.

"Then, there are the stories that people tell you at church. Write them down and throw them in your folder. You don't have to mention names - although on occasion you might want to do so when it relates to someone who has done something noteworthy that deserves praise. You can keep those for years and use them at any time.

"Anecdotes can also be found in books. You can record these in two ways. One is to use a photocopy machine. But I see you don't have one here."

"Too expensive," said Toblatt, who was making notes.

"Okay, well briefly write out the anecdote before you return the book to the library or a friend. If you have bought the book, note down the nature of the ancedote, the page number and name of the book and put that piece of paper in your anecdote file. When you need it, you can look it up in the book.

"Gather anecdotes from other sermons and talks , too. As long as the preacher is not in your own church, the chances are good your congregation will not have heard it. You should always acknowledge the source anyway.

"In time, you will build up a highly respectable source of illustrations that will serve you well.

"You will also find it really useful to illustrate the points you are making in your sermon with quotes.

"So I suggest you start another set of folders, this time marked Quotes. Every time you come across a good quote - in the newspaper, in books, on television, from what people tell you or you hear in other sermons and talks - clip it out or write it down and put it in one of the folders.

"Don't rely on your memory - for anecdotes or quotes. Keep them in those folders. Then they'll be there when you need them.

"Later, when you get a large number you might want to sort them into themes to make it easier to find a useful anecdote or quote."

Markew stood up and stretched his arms."Now all I want to do is to see your notes and then we are done for the day." Toblatt obliged.

The Opening

1. It must grab the reader's attention in 10 seconds.
2. The best hook is an example - an anecdote or scene-setter.
3. It should relate to the listener's life in a way that he or she can understand.
4. Seize the listener's attention before other thoughts can do so.

Illustrations

1. Fill the sermon with illustrations - anecdotes and quotes.
2. Keep the moralizing brief.
3. Start a folder for anecdotes and quotes. Gather them from:

a) Newspapers and magazines
b) Books
c) Conversations
d) Other sermons/talks

Master Plan

Toblatt wondered how Markew would arrive this time. It was just before 9 a.m. Thursday. And he was looking forward to the last lesson. He was even looking forward to preparing his sermon on Friday and putting what he had learned into practice. He wondered how the next poll would turn out.

Already he had clipped items of interest from the evening and morning newpapers. And he had in mind two sermon topics as a result of discussions with members of his congregation in the past two days.

He had to confess to himself that this was becoming exciting. He saw his challenge in a new light. No longer would he be content with simply outlining his ideas. He would now try to relate to the interests of his congregation, then jump into their minds and demand attention.

Suddenly Markew was there, holding up a large piece of paper on which a series of boxes had been drawn.

"Here's your master plan," said Markew. "It's

always easier to understand something when you see it sketched out like this."

This was the sketch he held up:

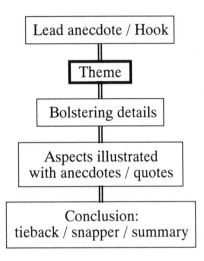

"We've talked about the lead and how you should grab the attention of your listeners right at the outset with a good story or something dramatic.

"I've called it a hook here as well because this is what people in television call it. It's also called a tease.

"You need to get your listeners tuned to your channel right at the start with a hook. And keep them tuned in - right through the commercials. You're competing with hundreds of other channels, in their minds.

"I've also spoken about the next step - the theme that summarizes what you are saying.

Everything revolves around that. That's what they're going to remember.

"And I've mentioned that you should use examples, in the form of anecdotes and quotes, to illustrate what you are saying. The best example should, of course, be used right at the start as the attention grabber.

"Today I want to move on from the theme and talk about compiling the main body of your sermon and the conclusion.

"The theme should be followed by what I've called bolstering details.

"This means that, after you have stated your theme, you set about bolstering, or supporting, it.

"Here's your chance for just a short - and I mean short - explanation. Say why you think the statement in your theme is important. In this case, say why you think we should worship the Lord wherever we might be, not just in church. You should quote a Bible verse or two to back up your argument.

"Indeed, this is the point at which you could introduce your text, which, of course, should be directly related to the theme. At times, your nut graph could be a summary of your text.

"And your Bible reading earlier in the service should ideally be directly related to the theme as well.

"Set aside only a minute or two for this. Now you've got their attention, you don't want to lose it.

Listeners are very adept at realizing when they are being told what to do - and for many that's a time to tune out.

"I remember when I ran a club for children aged from 8 to 11, I would often tell them a story with a moral. I would take, say, 10 minutes to tell a really exciting story and for that time I would have their undivided attention.

"When I concluded the story and reached the moral, they turned away, their feet shuffled and they were ready to get up and go. I found the most effective method to avoid the automatic turnoff was to make the moral an essential ingredient of the story.

"Children at that age tell you when they are bored. Adults don't. But the result is the same.

"After the bolstering details, you move on to the main body of the sermon. Let's go with that same example with which I started - we should worship the Lord outside of church as well as in it. Let's assume that in your research - and using your own ideas, of course - you have come up with three places in which we can worship.

"Let's say, for argument's sake, they are these: We should worship at home with our family; we should worship at work; and we should worship during our leisure time.

"Set aside a definite amount of time - let's say it's four minutes - to deal with each point. That will mean 12 minutes for the three main points, three minutes for the lead or hook, two minutes for the bolstering details, and three minutes for the conclusion. That's a total of 20 minutes. Quite long enough to get your points across. I would say no sermon should go beyond 20 minutes.

"Making it longer is as bad as writing a 40-inch story that looks so formidable when you see it stretched across the page you are put off reading it.

"Of course, you have the benefit that no one is quite sure how long your sermon is going to be. That's like starting a 40-inch story with 5 inches on Page One so your readers get into the story before they realize how long it is.

"But - make no mistake - there's a cutoff point. Like one of those timers that set the lights in a room to remain on for only so long, your listeners are going to turn you off automatically if you overstay your welcome in their minds. Remember, the kids tell you, the adults don't.

"The television and radio people say our attention span is 12 minutes. That's why radio news bulletins are seldom longer than that - usually they're only three or four minutes - and that's why TV shows usually have commercial breaks every 12 minutes.

"In our breakdown, the main body of the sermon, the aspects of the theme, lasts 12 minutes. This means that the opening part and the concluding section must be especially interesting so that they are divided off - almost like commercials divide up a TV show. That way you can keep their attention throughout the 20 minutes.

"So, having explained your theme, you move

on to the first point: We should worship at home.

"Find illustrations for that - from your own life if necessary. Throw in a bit of humor, too. That always helps.

"It's possible that at this stage of your preparation you will come up with an anecdote that is good enough for your lead, or hook. Don't hesitate to move it up there. If you have already chosen one that is weaker, move it down into the body of your sermon and move the better one into the opening slot.

"Let's say you started your sermon with an anecdote about how difficult it is to get a Bible reading going in your home because the TV is on and Johnny has to do his homework, and so on. Everyone can relate to that. You might brighten it with your own experiences.

"You then moved on to state your theme and provide a brief bolstering explanation. The next section is your first point - the first aspect of worshiping everywhere. At this stage, when you are explaining your first point, you could include anecdotes of people worshiping at home that will serve as examples.

"When your four minutes are up, move on to the next point. Don't be tempted to go on with the first point beyond the allotted time and cut into the next point. That puts your whole sermon off balance and you're going to bore your listeners with additional comments and lose them.

"You're going to be tempted to add one extra point that has just come to your mind while you're standing there. Then you want to add another, and so on.

"Don't.

"Stick to what you have prepared."

Markew held up the sheet of paper with the boxes on it again.

"You'll notice I've put one box for all of the aspects of the theme. This should really be three different boxes, as you deal with each aspect. But I've put one box on this paper as this is a master plan and sometimes you might have only two aspects and other times you have four.

"Remember, however, to adjust your time accordingly. Two aspects means you can take a little longer on each. But four means you must cut down on each.

"Having dealt with the first aspect of your theme - how we can worship at home - you move on to the next: How we can worship at work.

"Again, get in those illustrations. In your anecdote folder might be a story about a Christian who has risen to the top in a company and runs the place in a way that enables him to say he is worshiping the Lord as he runs the company each day.

"You could deal with the problems that most people face in trying to live like Christians at work. By not cursing and by keeping to Christian standards of honesty at work many people will, in effect, be worshiping. Tell this in the form of a story, or a parable. You could even make up a story, and say: What if this were to happen?

"Once again, I must emphasize that you should try to relate what you say to the average person in your congregation.

"Dealing with cursing at work is a constant problem for many. They don't want to know what the Greek is for an obscure word in Thessalonians. They want to know how to deal with the guys at work who mock them for being Christians. They want to know whether it is better to be a witness by simply doing what is right at work or whether one should tell all your fellow workers just what great sinners they are and warn them of the consequences.

"The third point could deal with which TV programs one should watch, which movies one should see and it could discuss creative use of leisure time, again with plenty of illustrations."

Markew paused.

"I'm sure you get the idea, Mr. Toblatt. You know how to divide up a sermon into various points. You know how to illustrate those points with quotes and examples.

· "The important thing is to do it. And to do it always.

"Don't allow yourself to slip back into the sloppy habit of simply outlining your three points as though you were dictating a Bible dictionary.

"Illustrate, illustrate and illustrate.

"By all means, of course, illustrate with stories and quotes from the Bible. The best stories are there. The best quotes are there.

"But include everyday stories, too. Relate what you can to the news of the day. Relate what you can to the activities of people in your congregation. Relate what you can to questions they have.

"That's what Jesus did.

"Repeat your theme as you progress through the sermon. Say it over and over so people remember it and realize how the other points fit in with it."

Markew stood up. "Now for the conclusion," he said.

"The conclusion of your sermon must be one of its best features. Prepare it as well as you have prepared every other aspect. You want to conclude with something that people will remember.

"The opening hook got their attention. It stopped their minds from drifting off into another world.

"The nut graph told them the theme of your sermon - what you are trying to tell them.

"The breakdown of the theme into various aspects illuminated the theme so that they understood it better.

"Now you want them to walk out with a final thought in their minds that will leave all the rest of the sermon imprinted in their memories.

"I'm going to suggest three ways in which you can do this. Again, they are based on devices used in the media.

"The one is the tieback.

"This means you refer again to the anecdote or scene setter with which you started.

"Using my example of worshipping wherever you are, you would go back at the end to that scene in your home where you are battling to have devotions against a sea of distractions.

"You might end the sermon by saying how you solved the problem. That will tie it all up nicely, like a ribbon on a gift-wrapped parcel.

"Make sure it's stated briefly. This is a conclusion, remember, not the elaboration of your theme. You've done that already. Keep it down to a minute or two.

"Another device to end a message is a summary. This can be a moral, telling your listeners what you hope they have learned today.

"It's a kind-of: So you see we should never do it this way, but we should always ... ending. But please, please don't make it sound like: The moral of this story is ... Say what you want to say succinctly. Like: You can worship at home, at work and at play. Wherever you are. At any time. In many different ways. Let's all aim to do that this week.

"Leave it at that.

"A third way to conclude is with the snapper.

"This is a bright, pithy statement that comes as a surprise to your listeners.

"An example is an article I read that starts with an anecdote of a woman who does a massive amount of work for charity. Only in the last paragraph do we find out that she is blind herself.

"Save your best statement for last. Surprise, or better still, shock your listeners.

"And then stop."

Toblatt had been writing notes and when he looked up Markew was no longer sitting in the chair opposite his desk. He had gone. He wanted to show Markew his notes, but now he could not do so. So he read them over himself. He was sure Markew would approve of them.

Bolstering details

State briefly what your theme is all about.
Introduce text.
Don't go on for too long.

Main body of sermon

Divide theme into two, three or four aspects. Preferably three. Spend about four minutes on each aspect. A total of 12 minutes.

Illustrate each aspect with examples and quotes.

The conclusion

End with a short remark with impact.

Devices:
1. The tieback - return to beginning
2. The summary or moral
3. The snapper - a short surprise

Acid Test

Toblatt was hoping for congratulations, of course. He felt the sermon had gone well. He had started with a dramatic illustration he had found in a news magazine, moving on to his theme and illustrating his points as he went.

He had kept the sermon to 21 minutes.

He had even come up with a surprise ending.

As he stood at the door he listened with greater than usual interest to the comments the members of his congregation were making.

Many said how much they appreciated the sermon. They even commented on the theme. Some said it would help them to cope with the demands of the week ahead at work. Others said it was the kind of problem they had been hoping he would discuss one day. Some wanted to discuss their problems with him later, during the week. Most had obviously understood the main points of his sermon.

Toblatt had looked around the congregation during the service to see if he could spot Markew. But he had not seen him. He had probably been sitting behind someone - or off in a corner somewhere. That seemed to be typical of the man. Toblatt was confident Markew would soon appear.

But as the line of people leaving the church drew to an end, he did not see him.

Perhaps he was outside, at the entrance polling the congregation, Toblatt thought. He was really interested to hear what the poll would find.

By the time he had shaken the last person's hand, Toblatt was wondering whether he had imagined the whole thing.

The last person in the line was Mr. Nalegan. A faithful church member, he seldom had anything to say about the sermon. Indeed, he seldom spoke at all. But he was always there, week after week.

"Good sermon," Nalegan commented as he shook Toblatt's hand. "I would say 92 percent of your listeners would remember what they heard today, at least as they were leaving the church. And probably 87 percent would say they learned something new. Keep it up. That's the kind of stuff we want to hear.

"My mind didn't wander. I could relate to everything you said. You didn't go on for too long as you sometimes tend to do."

Toblatt was so surprised he could not reply. He stared at Nalegan as he slowly walked off.

Had Markew been there, after all?

Toblatt guessed he would never know for sure.

ORDER FORM

Please send me the following items:

___ The Three Lessons of Mr. Markew
at $9.95 each
Washington state residents add $0.82 sales tax

$ _____

Shipping and handling: $3 per order
Outside the U.S. $5 $ _____

TOTAL DUE and ENCLOSED $ _____

Please enclose check or money order

Name: _____

Address: _____

City/state/zip: _____

Send order to:

LifeTime Creations,
33602 27th Pl. S.W., Suite 301
Federal Way, WA   98023-7711